I Can't Remember

Ella O'Connor desperately wants to tell a story, but every time she opens her mouth, her words disappear. Will she ever discover the joy of becoming a storyteller and unlock the secret that ideas and stories can be found everywhere?

This beautifully illustrated story book explores a common situation that arises for children and teachers taking part in Helicopter Stories, and allows the children to explore their feelings in a sensitive and supportive environment. The story is accompanied by teacher's notes on how to use the book with young children, along with questions and discussion prompts that can be incorporated into the curriculum.

In a class where Helicopter Stories take place on a regular basis, *I Can't Remember* offers an empowering solution for those moments when a child can't think of anything to say. It is part of the *Helicopter Stories Tale* series, a valuable and visually captivating resource for all Early Years educators using storytelling and story acting with their children.

Trisha Lee is a writer, theatre director and storyteller. She was the first to pioneer Helicopter Stories in the UK and she founded the theatre and education company MakeBelieve Arts in 2002.

Amie Taylor is a writer and artist. She founded her shadow puppetry and illustration company 'The Shadow Makers' in 2013 and now delivers workshops and projects in creating shadow work and illustration.

T0056243

"These picture books bring to life the magic of Storytelling and Story Acting. The authentic examples and quandaries are compelling. Trisha gives advice based on her vast experience but also includes the voice of Vivian Gussin Paley herself. This book will be an invaluable resource for anyone who is developing the art of Helicopter Stories in their setting."

Anna Ephgrave, author of five books around the topic of "Planning in the Moment"

"Childhood deserves to spend its days in an immersive world of story and make-believe, and yet again, Trisha shows us how. The rich possibilities she has created here enable an exploration, not only of Helicopter Stories, but of who we are in the kingdom of play. A true adventure awaits you within its pages.

Holding hands with Trisha's words are the wonderful illustrations of Amie Taylor, that turn up the dial of imagination and invite us in to story dream even more."

Greg Bottrill, author of Can I Go and Play Now – Rethinking the Early Years and School and the Magic of Children

"Trisha Lee has written a lovely, accessible set of stories that can be dramatized through the Vivian Gussin Paley method. It is set in the classroom of Fiona Fable, who knows that every child has a story inside them, and her job is to find a way to let those stories out.

These stories bring to light the importance of children being able to tell their stories right here and right now. It's a beautiful and natural way of allowing children to address their worries, share their ideas and catch a glimpse of their imaginations.

We have used this approach for many years at LEYF [London Early Years Foundation], and it has made us so much more alert to the power of storytelling. Everyone has a story, and this book gives you the tools to make this part of your daily life of any classroom. It tells the teacher to watch very carefully, and you will see the children's stories dancing through the air. It is joyful."

June O'Sullivan, CEO of London Early Years Foundation, and author of numerous publications about the Early Years

I Can't Remember

A Helicopter Stories Tale

TRISHA LEE ILLUSTRATED BY AMIE TAYLOR

Routledge
Taylor & Francis Group
LONDON AND NEW YORK

Cover image: Amie Taylor

First edition published 2023
by Routledge
4 Park Square, Milton Park, Abingdon, Oxon, OX14 4RN

and by Routledge
605 Third Avenue, New York, NY 10158

Routledge is an imprint of the Taylor & Francis Group, an informa business

British Library Cataloguing-in-Publication Data
A catalogue record for this book is available from the British Library

Library of Congress Cataloging-in-Publication Data
Names: Lee, Trisha, author. | Taylor, Amie, illustrator.
Title: I can't remember : a helicopter stories tale / Trisha Lee ; illustrated by Amie Taylor. Other titles:
    I cannot remember
Description: First Edition. | New York : Routledge, 2023.
Identifiers: LCCN 2022015742 (print) | LCCN 2022015743 (ebook) | ISBN 9781032053769 (Paperback) |
    ISBN 9781003197317 (eBook)
Subjects: LCSH: Learning strategies. | Language arts (Early childhood) | Language acquisition. | Memory. |
    Storytelling. | Literacy. | Children—Books and reading.
Classification: LCC LB1066 .L44 2023 (print) | LCC LB1066 (ebook) | DDC 372.6—dc23/eng/20220718
LC record available at https://lccn.loc.gov/2022015742
LC ebook record available at https://lccn.loc.gov/2022015743

ISBN: 978-1-032-05376-9 (pbk)
ISBN: 978-1-003-19731-7 (ebk)

DOI: 10.4324/9781003197317

Typeset in Antitled
by Apex CoVantage, LLC

For Vivian

I CAN'T REMEMBER

A HELICOPTER STORIES TALE

TRISHA LEE

ILLUSTRATED BY AMIE TAYLOR

David Fulton Book

Introduction

Helicopter Stories is based on the work of American kindergarten teacher and author Vivian Gussin Paley. It was pioneered in the UK by Trisha Lee and theatre and education company MakeBelieve Arts.

Helicopter Stories is, in theory, a simple approach; children tell their stories to an adult scribe, who writes their words verbatim on an A5 sheet of paper. These stories are then acted out around a taped out stage.

I Can't Remember is based on a real-life situation in an Early Years classroom. It shows how difficult it is for some children to begin telling a story, even when they really want to.

At the end of the book, you will find more information on the strategies we use to help children when they want to tell a story but suddenly freeze. You will also find a copy of Ella's story for you to act out with your class.

I Can't Remember is suitable for children aged 3 to 7.

Fiona Fable's classroom overflowed with stories.
You could find ideas for them in every

nook and cranny.

And the most brilliant thing of all,
was that everyone took it in turns to
make up their own story and act it out.
"You can find stories everywhere," said Ms Fable.
The children nodded, for they knew she was right.

All, that is, except Ella O' Connor.

Ella desperately wanted to tell a story.

She wanted to tell one so very much.

But every time she found an idea,

the story

wriggled away.

"Today will be different," Ella muttered to herself. When Fiona Fable asked who would like to tell their story, Ella waved her arm frantically, eager to have a go.

"Are you ready to tell me your story?" asked Ms Fable.

Ella nodded and skipped over to the carpet.

Joyfully, she opened her mouth.

But
no
words
came
out!

Ella tried again.
Nothing.

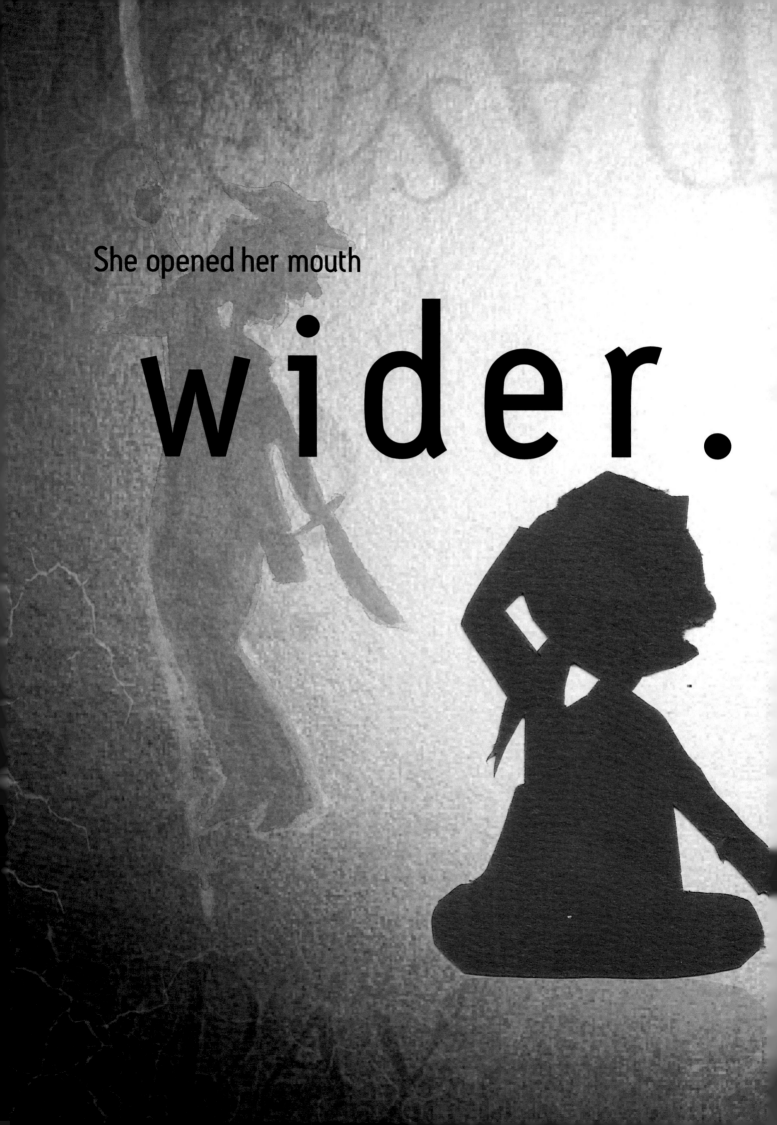

She opened her mouth

wider.

But still nothing came out.

Where had all her words gone?

"I can't remember," whispered Ella.

"It's okay," said Fiona Fable. "There's no rush."

Ella **thought.**

And **thought.**

And **thought.**

But every time she came close to grabbing an idea,
it disappeared before she could catch it.

Ms Fable waited a bit longer.

Ella thought a bit harder.

Waiting.   Thinking.

Waiting.   Thinking.

"Would you like someone to help you?" asked Ms Fable.

Ella tried to say "Yes", but only a

squeak came out.

Ms Fable invited some of the other children to come up with ideas.

"What character do you think might be in Ella's story?" she asked. "Dogs," said Daisy. "Ella loves dogs. I love dogs too. We could be dogs together!"

"It could be about dinosaurs," said Oliver.

"Stories with dinosaurs are the best."

"Maybe your story could be about a princess," said Ariana. There were always princesses in Ariana's stories.

But Ella didn't want to tell a story about a **princess,** or a **dinosaur** or a **dog**.

Ella looked around her. There was a story in her head a while ago, but now all her ideas had disappeared. She searched for them everywhere. Under the table, in the blocks, on the shelf near the home corner.

Then she noticed Dillan, the hamster, chewing on his cage, trying to escape.

"Once there was a hamster," said Ella.
"A naughty hamster. The police came to arrest
him. They put him in a cage, but he
nibbled a hole in the bars. Then he
ran home. What a naughty hamster!"

Ella sighed. She'd done it. She'd told a story.
Fiona Fable was right; you could find stories everywhere.

"When we act out my story, I want to be the hamster,"
said Ella, crawling away on all fours.

Teachers Notes - I Can't Remember

"Let's face it, what school usually does is continually interrupt any attempt on the part of children to recapture the highly focused intensity of play.
What we need to do is help them – and ourselves – to get back on track."

Vivian Gussin Paley – *The Girl with The Brown Crayon*

Once you have read *I Can't Remember* to your children, think about initiating a conversation with them, using some of the starting points below.

- I wonder what Ella felt like when she was sitting next to her teacher trying to think of a story. What do you think was going on in her mind?
- Have you ever wanted to tell a story, or say something to someone, then as soon as you opened your mouth, you completely forgot what you were going to say? What does that feel like?
- If you had to help one of your friends make up a story, what character would you suggest they include?
- Would there be different character ideas for different friends? Try thinking of some of the children in your class. What characters would they have in their stories?
- What do you do when you can't think of an idea for a story? Is there anything that might help you to come up with one?

Ask your children if they would like to act out Ella's story.

Ella's Story

Once there was a hamster. A naughty hamster. The police came to arrest him.
They put him in a cage, but he nibbled a hole in the bars. Then he ran home.
What a naughty hamster!

When you act out this story, take it in turns around the stage, just like they do in Fiona Fable's classroom. Ask the child playing the hamster how they think a hamster might move around the stage. This will encourage them to crawl like a hamster. Don't worry if it doesn't work and the child doesn't move. Their hamster might be a standing hamster. The children will start moving eventually. Just keep asking for actions and see where they take it. As well as asking children to play the police officers and the hamster, invite some of them to become the bars of the cage that the hamster is locked in. Let them work out how to do this, and remember that whatever they come up with is fine.

Here are some quick pointers to help with the acting out:

- Gather the children in a circle around a rectangular, taped out stage. Alternatively, get children to sit around the edges of your classroom carpet.
- Read the story, one line at a time, inviting individual children to become each character and act out that segment of the story before moving to the next sentence.
- At the end of the story, clap thank you, and everyone sits back down.

For more information on how to deliver Helicopter Stories, read Princesses, Dragons and Helicopter Stories by Trisha Lee, which is a how-to on the approach, or visit https://helicopterstories.co.uk/courses/helicopter-stories-on-demand/.

Sometimes when we open our mouths to speak, we forget what we were about to say. It happens to all of us. Even adults. Maybe the thought just disappears, and try as we might, we can't seem to bring it back. Alternatively, perhaps we are ready to add our thoughts to the conversation, but by the time we get our chance to speak, what we wanted to say feels less relevant, and we become self-conscious about saying it. I'm sure at some point all of us have said, "Oh, don't worry about it. It's not important. I can't remember."

Children, for the most part, are tremendous risk-takers. They will happily volunteer to participate in something without fully understanding what it involves. How many of us as adults are still prepared to do that? Ask any group of three- to six-year-olds, "Would any of you like to tell me a story?" Within seconds you will be staring at a sea of hands, all hoping desperately for their turn, even if none of them has ever told a Helicopter Story before. Many of these children will be happy to start making something up the minute you ask them.

But what about the ones like Ella in the story above? For Ella and children like her, the desire to tell a story is there. However, the minute they sit in front of their teacher, and it is their turn to speak, everything they had imagined they would say vanishes. In these moments, the child might look at the floor, or play with their fingers, or open and close their mouth, as if hoping that some words will come out. When I have been in this situation with a child, waiting silently for them to tell their story, I have often heard them mutter, "I can't remember."

For a long time, I was never sure what to do in these moments, torn between my desire to ensure that a child wasn't forced into telling a story when they didn't want to and not wanting them to feel like they had failed. I'd sometimes ask the child what character they'd like to be in their story, hoping this would spur them into action. However, if they shrugged and still didn't say anything, I didn't push it any further. Instead, I'd sit quietly. I might even say something like, "Are you having a think?" Then I'd nod and smile encouragingly. After a suitable waiting period, I'd say, "You can come back and tell me later if you like." The child would then jump up and run away, happy to be free from the silent prison.

I was never entirely on board with this way of doing things, but I wasn't sure what else I could do. I hoped that for these children, the experience of putting their hands up, of being asked to tell their story, of having their chance to sit next to me with my pen and paper poised, was enough for that moment. That they had experienced what it felt like when they agreed to tell a story, and at a later date, they would be ready to take it further.

For years this was the only strategy I had. I firmly believe that no child should be forced, coerced or bribed to tell a story. I would always check to make sure that my actions weren't making the child feel like they had to be there, but I hated seeing them so awkward and wished there was a way I could help.

As I worked with more and more children, I began to realise that the need to tell a story was so great in some of them, maybe too great, that this created the block. As I sat silently beside children like this, waiting, I could see their brains working away, trying to find that opening line so that they could tell their story. It is the oral equivalent of writer's block. Too many ideas pouring into the brain, and uncertainty about which is the right one to pick. Once I started to think about the situation in this way, telling a child they could come back later began to feel like failure.

I spoke to Vivian Gussin Paley about it. To my relief, she had a strategy that I had never heard of before—one that changed my practice. Like me, Vivian believed that turning a child away when they couldn't remember the story they wanted to tell was wrong. She spoke about this dilemma at a conference in Boston in 2012.

> *"What I will never do, is say, when a child wants to tell a story but is silent,*
> *we'll come back to you later. There is no later. The job of the teacher is to make it now."*

Vivian's strategy was to ask the other children in the room to help. As she described at the conference in Boston, she would turn to the group and say:

"Jessica has a story, but she can't quite remember it. Now, if I played with Jessica, I would make some suggestions as to what characters she likes to play, but you children play with her, and that's how you learn what is on your friend's mind. Jessica, would you like me to ask three people to give you an idea for a character you might like to tell a story about?"

Of course, Jessica said yes, and Vivian asked the children around the stage to suggest characters that might be in a story that Jessica would make up. Each idea was then offered to Jessica to use or reject. As soon I heard this strategy, I knew I had to try it. I am still amazed at how successful it is.

The first time I tried it, I was doing an INSET training session with some teachers, and I was delivering a demonstration with a group of children. There were twenty adults in the room and fifteen children. A girl called Sara put her hand up to tell a story, but she froze as soon as she sat down next to me. I had never tried Vivian's strategy before, but I knew I had to use it.

Sara opened her mouth. "I can't remember," she said.

"Do you want me to ask someone to help you?" I asked nervously, unsure of the result. Sara nodded. I turned to the other children. "I wonder if you can help me," I said. "Sara has a story that she can't remember. I don't play with her, so I don't know what characters might be in her story, but maybe you can help out. What sort of characters might be in Sara's story? What does she like?"

A boy put his hand up and said, "Elsa [from the movie *Frozen*]. Sara is always playing Elsa."

Sara nodded.

"And Anna," added the girl who was sitting next to him.

Sara nodded some more.

Another boy spoke. "She likes Beauty and the Beast too."

By this point, Sara was smiling widely, and I could tell that each of the characters her friends had suggested resonated with her.

"So, tell me, Sara," I said, "We've got Elsa, and Anna and Beauty and the Beast. Which one of these characters would you like to have in your story?"

I held my breath, waiting to see if Sara replied. She smiled and whispered, "Elsa."

I don't know who was more relieved, me or Sara. I wrote the word Elsa on my page. Sara looked at one of the girls and added, "and Anna." Then she muttered, "fell."

Having told her story, Sara scuffled back to her place around the stage, the biggest smile on her face.

"Elsa and Anna fell," I read the story to the group. It was Sara's story and a huge success.

When it came to the acting out, Sara skipped happily around the stage and then dramatically fell over at the story's climax. The other children laughed and laughed.

Inside, my heart fluttered, still unable to believe that it had worked. Rather than saying to Sara, "I'll do your story later," Vivian's approach was like magic, and Sara achieved her wish with the help of her friends.

From that moment onwards, I have always asked the child if they want some help. When the story is part of private storytelling, I ask them to fetch a few friends who might be able to help them, or we ask the friends who are sitting near them as they dictate their story. It never fails to produce a reaction. Knowing that your friends are aware of the things that are important to you can cut through any oral storytelling block.

But do remember, sometimes the story you get, maybe as a result of friends helping out, or from a child at the beginning of their storytelling journey, might just be one word or a short sentence like Sara's.

"Elsa and Anna fell" is the perfect beginning to a child's growth as a storyteller. Sara has introduced us to two characters, and then something happens; they fall over. This is the essence of all stories, there are characters, and something happens to them. As time goes by and Sara tells more stories, her novel will unfold.

If children believe they can succeed, that whatever they say will be accepted, and that if they are struggling, they can ask for help from a friend, then they will take more risks, and their confidence as storytellers will grow. We must always accept the word 'no', that if a child doesn't want to tell a story on that day, that they can walk away. But having another strategy that allows them to turn to their friends for help opens up this activity in an exciting way. There will always be a fine line between supporting and leading, between interacting and interfering, but by inviting the children to help each other, each child is made to feel safe, even when they can't remember.